It's Never Too Late to Be GREAT!®

FINDING THE SPARK WITHIN YOU THAT SETS YOU ON A PATH TO GREATNESS

BERNADETTE GREGGORY

© 2023 - Bernadette Greggory

All rights reserved. This book is protected by the copyright laws of the United States of America. No part of this publication may be reproduced in any form without prior written permission from the publisher.

Printed in the United States of America.

Cataloging-in-Publication data for this book is available from the Library of Congress.

ISBN: 978-0-9662049-6-4

DEDICATION

To my mother, Caroline. You were always in my corner, even when we lived so far apart. You always believed in me, even when it was hard for me to believe in myself. I will always remember your love and compassion. You are in my heart forever.

TABLE OF CONTENTS

Introduction 1
Foreword 7
Chapter One: Where Does Greatness Begin? 11
Chapter Two: The Spark 15
Chapter Three: You Can Do It! 17
Chapter Four: Why Am I Here? 19
Chapter Five: The Best Laid Plans 21
Chapter Six: Every Action is Capable of Changing the World 23
Chapter Seven: Others Can Hold You Back 25
Chapter Eight: You Are the Most Important Person in Your Life! ... 29
Chapter Nine: Looking Back 31
Chapter Ten: Greatness Shows up When You Do 33
Chapter Eleven: Inside-Out Greatness 37
Chapter Twelve: Are You Doing What You Love? 39
Chapter Thirteen: Who Can You Turn To? 41
Chapter Fourteen: The Healing Process 45
Chapter Fifteen: The Voice of God Whispers to Our Sacred Hearts. 49
Chapter Sixteen: Be an Example 53
Chapter Seventeen: Where Did I Put My Life? 55
Chapter Eighteen: Can I Get Some Help Over Here? 59
Chapter Nineteen: When Do You Know? 63
Chapter Twenty: Just Lucky, I Guess? Guess Again. 67
About the Author 72

INTRODUCTION

My life story began in the middle. It was like a book you open up to a random page and start reading whatever words your fingers land on.

When I first wrote "It's Never Too Late to be Great!" it was because I wanted to share part of my story with others who had abandoned their dreams because they reached a certain age or encountered what seemed to be an insurmountable life trauma. It was an audiobook then. I created training classes around the premise and taught workshops based on the philosophy.

You see, I don't think people should abandon their dreams because of a life event that may not even have anything to do with the fulfillment of their dreams.

Dreams are related to your passion and purpose in life. They are born out of who you are. When you stop being who you are, or never discover your true essence, your dreams can fade and eventually disappear altogether.

But it doesn't have to be that way. I did a lot of things the hard way and paid some heavy prices for the wisdom I gained. I am happy for what I learned in this life, but the road could have been easier. I resisted plenty of ideas and resources that could have made things flow more smoothly.

I started college in my thirties and finished when I was forty. I worked in healthcare, education, and contract jobs through my small business. Most of my energy was spent on jobs where other people had control. My own business seemed to get closer and closer to the bottom of my priority list as I allowed others to control my destiny.

One day, when I had heard "You should have started sooner. You'll never be able to finish college". I'd just quit if I were you, all you do is study", and "Why do you feel you need to get a degree anyway?" one too many times, I'd had it. "Shut up!" I said loudly. "Do you see an expiration date stamped on my forehead? I'm doing this because I have dreams. I have goals. And I don't care how long it takes me. I'm going to do it." And I walked out.

My unexpected response even shocked me. "I need to write about this," I thought. So I did.

I'd had a successful medical radio talk show for two years and I have a good voice. So, instead of creating a book, I decided to create an audiobook. I had an idea of how I could use the audiobook as the base for personal empowerment training classes. It was all very inspiring at the time.

Then one day, while preparing to give a talk at a Women's Show in Topeka, KS, I had a terrible fall on a concrete floor. I was staying the night at my mother's house since she was close to the venue. I tried to play it down. It was the first time I would be a guest speaker at this type of event and I didn't want to give up now. Unfortunately, the trauma was too much and I was transported to the local hospital.

The young doctor there misdiagnosed the head trauma as a heart attack and I was air-lifted to a hospital a couple of counties away and admitted. I still had hopes of being able to make it the women's show to speak and staff my "Meet the Author" booth. Even after the cardiac cath showed that it hadn't been a heart attack, further tests were ordered. By the time I left the hospital, I was in excruciating pain from the untreated head and spinal injuries, and presumably, due to the additional test they performed, my heart rate was now double its normal 58 beats per minute.

Those were the days when health insurance wasn't mandatory and, since I didn't have any, I couldn't be transported to a trauma center once I had been discharged from the heart hospital. I drove to my hotel in Kansas City where I was part of a computer training team and did my job as best I could.

My dream of writing and public speaking was no more. The head trauma created so much pressure that I couldn't fly without unbearable pain. The day job that allowed me to finance my dream of writing and training my own classes based on my philosophy and life experience was gone. I traveled 100% of the time with my job, and I could no longer travel.

I had no home since the plan was to live at my mother's house, travel from there, and build my business alongside the computer training job which made it financially feasible. I returned to Florida where I had lived previously and stayed in a friend's apartment while she was in Germany.

An MRI revealed a mass behind my left eye. I could not read more than a few words without vomiting. I couldn't sing. I forgot how to spell. I was nauseated all the time, and the new problem with my heart seemed to have sealed my fate. A well-known cardiologist in the Tampa Bay area told me that I would probably not live two years without a pacemaker. I knew it was just me and God now.

In one of my more lucid moments during that ordeal, I stared at myself in the mirror. "Humph, no expiration date", I thought. I had lost a lot of my memory, but I remembered that.

It took a few years to get back to writing, narrating, and teaching again. It was pretty scary at the time. But that's how I share my gifts with the world, so I couldn't give up. And I didn't. I'm still here, and I'm still me, the crazy, out-of-the-box thinker and do-or-die dreamer, living inside-out and doing my darndest to take it all the way. It's been twenty years since the cardiologist made that prediction.

I cherish my morning walks and talks with God. I meditate and follow my intuition. Staying connected to God and the Universe allows me to enjoy the moments as they come. Each day I wake up to new possibilities and new dreams filled with joy and adventure. I rather expect that will continue for as long as I live.

And it all started the day I allowed myself to believe that It's Never Too Late to be Great!

FOREWORD

About twelve years ago, I started my adult journey to fulfilling my God-given purpose when I started a position at a local radio station in Tampa, FL. I was invited to a networking meeting at a public library in Brandon, FL. I was just a few years out of college and remember being the youngest person in the group.

We all had to tell who we were and what we did. At that time I had recently joined a community television station with the dream of becoming a big-time television producer. Bernadette introduced herself as a coach and motivational speaker who wanted a new direction in life. I can't remember too many details from that night, but I remember this woman had so much passion and energy for her vision. I'd never met anyone who dreamed in 3D like me. She didn't look like me, we didn't come from the same place; we weren't the same age, but our energies and zeal tied us at that moment.

Throughout the years, we kept in contact. Sometimes a few years would pass until we spoke but the energy was always the same. We would talk about the obstacles in our way and the provisions we were made to push through. And every time we talked, she always gave me a resource to help me with a problem I was facing.

Around the time I was graduating from a master's program, she gave me her CD "It's Never Too Late to Be Great!" I listened to the whole CD. As I listened, the words were so comforting. It was like going to your favorite auntie's house and being welcomed with milk and a slice of freshly baked apple pie while sitting on an oversized comfy couch with your feet dangling off the edge like a kid. Her words were kind and full of compassion, but you walk away with the incredible feeling that, yes, I can overcome any trouble that comes my way.

To the corporate world, Bernadette was known as an energetic motivational coach with a relentless drive to motivate and empower any person, regardless of their age or background, who believes that greatness is within their reach. But I personally know Bernadette as an energetic motivational coach with a relentless drive who has motivated and empowered me for many years to continue to reach for that personal greatness that is on the inside of me.

We live in a world that can be harsh and supercritical towards people who want to pursue their dreams and personal greatness. They will judge you and tell you you're too old, the goal is unreachable, you're worthless, give up, you've been going at this too long and you still have nothing.

This is the moment where you retreat to your safe place and listen or read through the pages of her book, and allow her words to heal and transform you and give you the motivation you need to keep going.

—Krystal Brown, M.Sc.

Krystal Brown is the author of *Flip Yourself in 28 Days: Bounce Back and Start Living the Life You Dream About*, owner and President of KararD Multimedia Productions in Atlanta, GA, and Founder of Big Boned Fitness.

CHAPTER ONE
WHERE DOES GREATNESS BEGIN?

What is greatness, anyway? Where does it begin? How does it all start? Greatness begins where we do. We all start out in this nice, soft, cushiony safe body of water, where all of our needs are automatically and immediately met—food, water, shelter. It's a safe world that comes to an abrupt halt, when most of us are yanked or forced out into a loud, glaring, cold, sterile and strange outer world.

Our parents may or may not get to spend a moment with us before we are whisked away by strangers in frightening costumes who peer over their masks at us. They put drops in our barely opened eyes. They poke and prod, snip and slice, wash, dry and wrap us, often with very little verbal contact. Then they place us alone in a tiny bed in a large, ominous room, where all we can hear is the sound of monitors, and the collective horror of our own cries mingled with those of our tiny peers.

And so the fear begins. There's a grave misconception that what happens to us as children we naturally forget. You know, when we're very, very little, we know more than you might think.

While still inside the womb, we are safe and free at the same time. In most cases, we want for nothing, and we feel very self-sufficient, in the manner of speaking. But now we're in this new outside world where we must depend on other human beings for every single thing we want and need. We can think. We have all the consciousness of soul, that Divine spark of love, the spark of God we have within us. But unfortunately, we are not able to do much with it because the new body we now have is too inexperienced to act on these needs.

So, as time goes on and the self-discovery process works in its normal way, our dreams, desires, and expectations are refined. They are adapted and they are adjusted, according to the consciousness we have as a small child. Because children construct their world in a way very different from adults, concepts and ideas are mixed together, interfaced in a way similar to the way a computer processes data. The computer can logically plot out and extrapolate information in a way that an infant or a small child is not able to.

Added to this, we have emotions. So now we have this mind that is just beginning to process, just beginning to grow and grasp, taking in everything around it with all its five senses, learning more than 80% of everything this little being will know in its entire life—before it is five years old. And we're adding emotions.

In the outside world, we feel needy, and being needy makes us feel afraid. Without even realizing it, living in the present moment of a child's tender heart, we learn fear as we seek the approval of our caretakers so that they will provide what we need for our survival. Our world, which once consisted only of us, must now be opened up to strangers if we are to have our needs met, if we are to survive.

During the first two years of life, learning to trust is our primary task. If our parents are there to fulfill our basic needs of food, clothing, shelter, and love, then we will expect this outcome. As a result, we will feel safe enough to journey out on our own attempting to meet our own needs in our own adventurous ways. As long as we believe that help will be there when we need it, we can move ahead with our learning without worrying about how we will survive.

CHAPTER TWO
THE SPARK

Everyone has "the spark" when they come into this world. Within our hearts are sown the seeds of greatness. But it is up to us to cultivate them, to bring them to maturity, and to harvest them into the essence of who we are. What gets us to this point? The point where we decide that greatness is something we want to have in our lives?

For some people it happens at a young age, twenty or thirty years old. A few of us know from the very beginning as young children what we will do with our lives, what we will accomplish in a particular occupation, hobby, or sport. I often hear people say, "I'll be great at whatever I do". It's a wonderful attitude, but it isn't always enough. In order to do great things, we need to involve other people. Greatness happens when sharing and trusting, giving, and just being, happen. Greatness happens when we reach outside of our comfortable circle into other places, and to other people, and accept them into our hearts. We need to accept them into our consciousness, accept even the things that we may not understand about them. We learn and grow from the experience of being around them, just as they will learn and grow from the experience of being around us.

These are not people who hurt you, put you down, or dash your dreams with the negativity of their own feelings of inadequacy. The people you want around you are the people who accept you for who you are. Those who offer unconditional love, compassion, acceptance, and respect for your experiences which have made you the person you are. Greatness happens when you happen to life.

Greatness is without limitations but is not achieved without boundaries, which guide you on your right path. There is really no limit to the number of things an individual can do to make a difference in this world, and a difference in his or her own life. These individual accomplishments are wonderful. They make us feel like we're special, separate, better than, because we've done a special thing or accomplished a special goal. There is nothing wrong with wanting to be special, to feel important, to feel respected and loved.

Most of the things we do to promote greatness come from the outside in. It simply is the way we've been conditioned and socialized in our upbringing. True greatness comes from the inside out. It is a magnet of dynamic energy that attracts all to it, and makes the impossible possible. When you feel it, there is no doubt in your mind that it has come from who you are, the Inside You, the Perfect You.

CHAPTER THREE
YOU CAN DO IT!

We're like the fragile petals of a rose, slowly unfolding to expose the beauty within. We struggle in silence, in the darkness, traveling underground, searching for a crack in the concrete, a tear in the moss, any opportunity to spring up and share our beauty with the world.

No one knows of our journey, how far we traveled, or the difficulties we have encountered. They see only the open flower, the finished product. They do not know who we are, and sometimes we don't want to remember where we've been. And so we forget, and look to the outside for answers we can find only from within.

Eventually, we come to a place in our lives when we must face a monster far more challenging and far more frightening than anything else we have ever faced. The monster we must confront is the one we see in the mirror.

We cannot hide the truth from ourselves, nor do we really want to. It takes great courage to tell the truth, especially to ourselves. Feelings, even though they are only in our minds, often block the way to our greatness.

CHAPTER FOUR
WHY AM I HERE?

Who am I? What am I all about? What is my place in this life? What is my purpose? Always more questions. Why is there never enough time to rest and reflect? Why don't I feel that I belong anywhere? How the world sees you is not as important as how you see yourself. When you know who you are, you are free to belong anywhere you want. You will have earned the right. You have it now. It's just a matter of recognizing that your greatness, your real power, comes from within you. It's right there in that beautiful heart of yours.

You can be just about anything that anyone else would like for you to be. People do it all the time. We are like chameleons. It's a learned skill that becomes a confusing game, and after a while, life's not fun anymore. In our personal relationships, we often expect our partners to be psychic. Our jobs take precedence over our families, and relaxation becomes something else we should do. We get so busy doing instead of just being that life passes us by. We don't stand still long enough for Life to notice us, to welcome us.

But life has its requirements. We have to work for a living, and that doesn't leave much time for anything else. And the new golden rule, "Whoever has the gold makes the rule", is always there to remind us that we are in second place. But there's no job security anywhere anymore, so what difference does it make where you go? And what difference does it make where you work? You might as well do something that you like, and bring your own brand of personal greatness to your job. So, go out there and find something you love to do. Happen to life. It happens to you. Happen to it for a change.

Position yourself so that you can draw good things to yourself, the kind of things you want in your life. Greatness is everywhere. It's never too late to be great! You are not alone. Life has not passed you by. Your time has not run out. There are plenty of chances left. And your name is written all over them.

CHAPTER FIVE
THE BEST LAID PLANS

What did you think you would be doing now when you were twenty? How about when you were thirty? Forty? Fifty? And have you done them or are you doing them now? Are you doing those things you once dreamed of doing, or did they get lost along the way? Do you ever think about them? Do they still call to you? Do you dismiss the idea when it pops into your head as something that was not meant to be?

You can still make those dreams come true. Oh, maybe not in the same way you could when you were twenty or thirty years old, but you're not the same person you were then. And who would you rather be right now?

Lighten up. It's okay to take a stand for something you believe in - YOU. Yes, you! Believe in yourself. Believe in your own greatness, and be who you were meant to be, unafraid to live the life of your dreams. Cherish the things that are important to you. Happen to Life. And don't ever give up! What you want in life and what you want out of life will change many times, and in many ways during the course of your existence on this planet. You will probably need to change too.

Of course, you will. We all resist it but in the end, most changes turn out better than we expected, and they feel more natural, more real. Sometimes you won't want to change, and other times you won't be able to, at least not right then. There will also be times in your life when you will welcome the change and the excitement it brings. Then there are those times when we feel that we just can't take on any more. God knows what we can handle, and we will never get more than what we're capable of getting through, even though it sure feels that way sometimes. Just hold on tight and put one foot in front of the other. And remember.......... It's Never Too Late to Be Great!

CHAPTER SIX
EVERY ACTION IS CAPABLE
OF CHANGING THE WORLD

Our relationship with God and the Universe is a very personal, very intimate connection. Everything we do influences our universe. We are all energy here. An idea is not created, a word is not spoken, a thought does not cross our minds that does not change our world in some way. This is the magnificence and the true miracle of life. Every act is capable of raising the consciousness of the world. What power we have in our hands! And what awesome responsibility!

We can come from abundance, or we can come from lack. We can come from love, or we can come from fear. When we are on purpose, life is good. Things just feel right. We are connected. We are great and we know it. We can feel it throughout our entire being. It's our game and we are calling the shots, but it's God's ballpark, so don't get too carried away. Love will always win out over fear. It's those extra innings that keep us on the edge of our seats, and on the edge of our lives.

CHAPTER SEVEN
OTHERS CAN HOLD YOU BACK

I'm almost embarrassed to recall some of my learning experiences, and how often they were repeated until I figured out what was going on and finally got the message. I've worked for people, men and women, who were so consumed by pathological lack that it came out in everything they did, and injured almost everyone they touched. The absence of love in their lives was profound and incomprehensible. It was a sad thing to witness, but my exposure to their disease helped me to recognize my own. I was trying to *do* my best in situations where I was not allowed to *be* my best. You can't have one without the other, so I learned what was really important in life. And they weren't it. And as long as I was around them, neither was I.

I was ready for something different. I began to change the way I thought about things. I learned different strategies and things began to change for me. I no longer looked to someone else to tell me what my heart had already told me years ago. I was finally ready to be me. Not to *do* anything, just to be me. It took me a long time to get there but I eventually stopped trying to figure everything out and started learning to accept the way things were at the moment.

I would like to say a few words about people I call PLTs (People Like That), because we have all experienced them. Maybe we were like that ourselves at some point in our life. These PLTs feel they do not have control over their lives, and so they compensate by attempting to control the lives of others. Most of the time, they don't see that this is what's really going on, and they leave a wide trail of broken hearts and shattered dreams in their wake. If they can control you, if they can get a reaction out of you, they can steal your personal power, and claim it for their own. But what usually happens is that we don't wait for them to steal it. We just hand it over to them.

When we don't know what is expected of us, we don't always know how to stand up for ourselves against this kind of emotional assault. When it happens in the workplace and threatens our livelihood, it's easier to take it. Not really easier, but that's what we tell ourselves. You can never please PLTs because they cannot accept themselves. They are not perfect enough. Of course, no one is except God, but they haven't figured that out yet. And, because they can't accept themselves for who they are, they can't believe that anyone else can either.

So they judge others by their own convoluted standards, which of course no one will ever meet, including them. Sometimes they make you their "whipping boy", and then try to convince you and themselves that they are actually helping you. This is a way of thinking much like an adult who beats a child tries to convince him or herself, that it will make the child a better person. It simply doesn't happen that way. PLTs are out of control people. It's not your job to save them. Save yourself. Get out of there. Get back to your life.

CHAPTER EIGHT
YOU ARE THE MOST IMPORTANT
PERSON IN YOUR LIFE!

Who is the most important person in your life? YOU! You are the most important person in your life. If you're not good for yourself, you won't be good for anybody else. That's just the way it is.

I was standing in front of a mirror one morning, robotically brushing my hair. I don't even think I actually noticed myself there. My mind began to drift into fantasy and I saw myself writing music again. I began feeling inspired and energized. And, in that moment of total relaxation, completely removed from my mundane job, and just dreaming for a moment, I realized something.

I had spent half my life trying to prove to people who didn't care about me that I could be something that I didn't want to be, in jobs that I pretty much hated. What a revelation that was! Sure I made the jobs work for me, but I rarely loved going to work in the morning. I just did it because it was my job and I needed it to survive. I always did my best, but it wasn't always what I really wanted to do. Once I was able to admit this to myself, my life began moving forward again. One day, one of my coworkers advised me that the boss was in a terrible mood. She warned me to stay out of the boss' way. The boss was one of those PLTs I talked about earlier. I looked at my colleague and I said, "God is my boss. I'm only on loan to her, and if she screws it up, then God will put me somewhere else where I'm needed and appreciated more."

And that's the way it eventually happened. We are not alone in this thing called Life. The PLTs who hurt us, and try to squash us like little bugs, because they don't like the way we look or dress, or we are too skinny, or we are too fat, or we are too much like them, do it because of who they are. It has nothing to do with us.

They are here to make us stronger, and stronger, and stronger until we finally stand up and say, "That's it, I'm outta here. I'm going to do something with my life that I really want to do." It's another way of saying, "I'm great, and I deserve better." Because you are, and you do. Once you believe you deserve better and start acting like it, your life will change for the better. Believe it or not, most changes *are* for the better. Life changes because we change, and it changes constantly. When the way we look at our life changes, life gets bigger and better and more fun. That's when we happen to life. That's when we know that it's never too late to be great!

CHAPTER NINE
LOOKING BACK

It's hard to move forward without looking behind once in a while. We need to look back to see how far we've come; to accept all the things that have happened to us, and be okay with them. We have to look back so we can let go and move forward.

I can't undo all the negative things that happened to me in my life, but I can heal them. If they hadn't happened, I couldn't do that. I wouldn't know how. I would miss the many wonderful experiences I'm now able to enjoy because of the enlightenment those negative experiences brought me. The joy that came with the enlightenment is one of the things that make life worth living for me. There's a line in the song from a Steven Sondheim musical that says, "Ignorance is bliss, but think of what you miss. "That pretty much sums it up for me.

CHAPTER TEN
GREATNESS SHOWS UP WHEN YOU DO

Greatness always happens in the same place, and always at the same time. That place is here, and that time is now. Greatness only happens in the present moment but the moment lasts forever. Don't let fear sneak up on you when you think about this. Every second of every day is an opportunity for greatness. Your now and your here is going to depend on the timing of your life and God's timing.

When all these little pieces to the puzzle of your life are gathered together, you can stand back and take in the whole picture. As the pieces are assembled, a plan will begin to emerge. Things will start to make sense. The fear is not so great when you see what kind of resources you have to work with. You can put a plan together. This is what I need, this is what I have; this is where I'm going. No, I've been there, I don't think that's for me right now.

Then the really big steps. I need help with this. I need help with that. Who can I call? Who can I ask? Who can I tell? Who *do* you tell your dreams to? How many times have you gone to somebody and said, "I have this great idea" and told them all about it. And they said, "It'll never work." What happened there? All the energy you built your dreams with—maybe it took years to get to the point where you really believed and felt confident enough to share your dream with someone whom you trusted to support you. All of that energy dissipated in less than a minute.

What were you thinking? Now you have to start over. It's okay because something is different now. Do you know what it is? Even though it feels like you're back to square one, you're not really. You've been there and done that. It's not going to take another fifteen or twenty years to nurture that dream again. You can pick up where you left off.

And what have you learned? First of all, you've learned that you *can* do it. And you've learned that you've got the guts to tell somebody about it. Those are big things, great things. And you've also learned that's one person you're never going to share your dreams with again. No, not even if they apologize. You see, it's an energy game, and they've tipped their hand. You can still be friends, but save the sharing for someone who believes in dreams like you do and will respect yours.

Now since you've already been down that road, you have a trail to follow. It's been said that if you're going down a path that's already there, then it's not your path, it's somebody else's. That makes sense because most of us are pioneers in our hearts. When it comes to getting what we really want, we can be very creative. Besides, even if we do travel a road that someone else already traveled, there's no guarantee we will meet the same fate as the person who originally hacked out the path.

We can take many roads to get to one place, or we can take one road to get to many places. GPS has proved that time and time again. As long as we arrive at our destination, we have taken the path that was right for us. Use your imagination and be lovingly persistent, and you can reach just about any goal you set for yourself. You can follow the road, change lanes, drive fast or slow, get off at an exit or take a side trip and get back on the road. You can travel on a super highway or an interstate, or a backwoods dirt road. You can even blaze your own trail if that's what you need to do to reach your destination. It's up to you. Once you can accept that these choices are yours to make, in some form or another, the journey can become very exciting!

CHAPTER ELEVEN
INSIDE-OUT GREATNESS

How do you answer people who ask you what you're really great at? Do you get embarrassed? And fumble for something to say? Do you say, "Well I'm great at tennis", or "I love chess, I have to say I'm pretty great at that." "Lots of things. Who wants to know?" For most of us, unless we've won an award or trophy or some outside kind of honor that proves by someone else's standards that we deserve the rating of "Great", we may not really know how to answer that question. None of these accolades or accomplishments actually *make* us great. We do that all by ourselves. There are established standards we have to live up to in order to earn the rating that has become the norm among people in the know. Some of those people won't be able to meet their own standards. It is a judgment, after all. But it is also something to aspire to. One is being and one is doing. Both are good and both flourish with support and encouragement.

I have a personal guideline that I'll share with you. I don't expect people to be more than they are, but I won't encourage them to be less.

If you're struggling to find your purpose in life, think about this. Whatever you do best, and whatever you love to do most, so much in fact that you would do it for free just for the pleasure it gives you, is directly related to your purpose here on this Earth.

Rest assured, if you follow your heart, greatness won't be far behind. A loving and compassionate heart will help you share your special gift with the world. You'll also need a healthy sense of humor and more flexibility than you can imagine. One thing is certain. Your life will turn out however it needs to turn out for you to learn the lessons you have come here to learn.

Many of the goals we achieve in our lives are occupation driven. We spend most of our waking hours at work, so I guess that makes sense. But there is so much more to life, and you deserve to have the best life you can get. So if you're going to get a life, you might as well get a great one.

CHAPTER TWELVE
ARE YOU DOING WHAT YOU LOVE?

I always wanted to be a writer and I've always written since I was a little girl. We get glimpses of our purpose all throughout our lives, little hints that this is something special, this is a gift. This is what we were put on this Earth to do. But we don't think about it like that. You know, we have our whole lives ahead of us and, in the excitement of youth, we put these absolutely critical pieces of information aside somewhere in our body and mind. And that's where they stay until some traumatic or otherwise life-altering event chokes up the past and reminds us of our buried treasure.

When I was in high school, Psychology and English were my two favorite subjects. I loved to write. For English composition, I would write these romantic, esoteric short stories. My teacher was touched by them. I knew this because she gave me A's on papers that I later discovered had several spelling errors. Once I noticed a smudge in the ink in a line in one of my stories that appeared to have caused by a teardrop. I was thrilled, even though that and the line, "Tommy was quite dead", are the only things I remember about that particular story.

My teacher had noticed what was important to me. She liked my work, and after all, she was an English teacher, an expert. I was great, and I knew it. What a wonderful sensation that was! And we didn't have to turn our papers back in, so she never saw the spelling errors. That was great, too.

We have so much to share with each other. Why don't we? The only way we ever take the good we have and make it into something great is to share our knowledge and wisdom with others. Everyone is knowledgeable; everyone is wise. No one on earth has cornered the market on knowledge and wisdom. Knowledge plus experience equals wisdom. And wisdom sometimes comes at a high price. The thing to remember is that the price of wisdom will never be greater than its value. Sometimes we confuse how much something costs with what it's worth. What something costs is measured by what we have to give up to get it. Value, or what something is worth, is what we see when we look at what we will gain. Either way, the risk is exactly the same. It's a coin toss. And it's your call.

CHAPTER THIRTEEN
WHO CAN YOU TURN TO?

If we don't depend on ourselves, who can we depend on? We think we know how we would take care of ourselves, what we would do………….. if. But the fact of the matter is, you really never know what you can do until you do it, and you do it, and you do it, and you fail, and you regroup, and do it again, and it bombs, so you change strategies, and you do it again, and it works.

Every single time we do something that doesn't work out the way we plan, we have three opportunities. We can accept the failure and say, "Forget it", and give up altogether. We can go on to a totally new project. We can explore other possible avenues for our present project: reinvent it, change our minds, look at it from a different perspective, take a different tact and make it work.

We always have options and opportunities. If we can just stand back far enough to see them, they will unfold before our eyes. First failures, by the way, are very common. It's just that the word doesn't get out to the commoners until years, decades, or even centuries have passed, and everyone who would've been embarrassed by the failures has died. But we know they happen all the time. Just consider all the wonderful inventions that were tried hundreds and thousands of times before they worked; the electric light, the automobile, the telephone, the toilet, the airplane, the camcorder, the television, the computer, and GPS, just to name a few.

If we can re-examine or reinvent an idea, why is it such a stretch of the imagination to think that we can reinvent ourselves? Why can't we start over with the knowledge and the enlightenment we have now, but with a fresh perspective? Can you think of what you might do now, at this stage of your life, if you decided to start over? You might want to consider continuing your education. What else would you like to know? What would you like to try next? Learning is an ongoing event. There is always something to learn that can enrich your life, sharpen your senses, or just be fun. When you are an adult in the educational system, there are so many opportunities open to you that I cannot begin to describe them. There are colleges that exist with the sole purpose of teaching adults in ways that are meaningful, and that reflect the reality, not just the theory, of living.

Everyone needs a life plan, not something chiseled in stone, but a flexible, malleable, doable plan that fits into your life and will work for you. Look at all the options, all the pieces. It's not enough to just survive. Let me qualify that statement. It's not enough for me just to survive. I want to be the best I can be every moment of my life. That means healing all the wounds, old and new, that keep me from living in the here and now and experiencing every moment as it comes.

When you get in touch with your greatness, you will find that the here and now, becomes the here and WOW. Life can be quite an adventure when you're connected—to yourself, to God, and to the Universe. Above all else, life is a spiritual journey, the greatest and most exciting journey you will ever make, and healing is an important part of this lifelong quest.

CHAPTER FOURTEEN
THE HEALING PROCESS

There are three steps in the healing process. They are like three different people we carry around with us. We learn from our healing, and we heal from our learning. Life is a spiritual experience, a road we must travel to find our connection, to reconnect with ourselves and our universe, and with God. The connection is never broken. We might forget about it sometimes, because it's an inside thing, and we live outside lives most of the time. But it's always there for us. It whispers to us, beckoning us to walk through. That door never closes, no matter what we think, feel, or do. However, it is a door that opens inward. If we push against it, resisting its call, it will seem that it cannot be opened. If we stand back and pay attention, we will see that we need to pull the door open to receive the blessing.

This is how we happen to life, instead of resisting everything, thus allowing life to happen to us. If we want to happen to life, we must learn to live inside out. This starts with accepting all the bits of who we are, even the ones that we don't want to see. It's all part of the healing process, the very thing that will set you free as the

Truth of your life is set free to flow like the greatest of oceans. It is that same Truth that will lead you home.

The healing process goes something like this: First, we are the Victim. It happens to all of us, God bless us, everyone. Even though we don't want to admit it, we've all felt like victims because we've all *been* victims of people and circumstances we cannot control. When we recognize that fact, we take the first step, and one of the most difficult, in the healing process.

We were victims because we got scared. We forgot about the power of love and we let fear in and we became helpless. Sometimes we didn't have any choice in the matter. We were helpless to change the way things were. So now we have to change our mind, and the way we think about what happened. We need to feel the fear, and the anger, and the shame, and all the feelings, so we can let them go. That doesn't mean we will never think of them again, but when we do, it won't hurt like it used to hurt. When we let go of how the experience made us feel, the pain will go away. When we set the terrible feelings free, let them go, we can be who we are, who we were always meant to be.

The second role we play in the healing process is that of the Survivor. We faced our fear, our victimization, and sometimes revictimization. We've come to see our attackers, abusive parents, thoughtless peers, ruthless business people, rapists, thugs, and all the other PLTs for what they are—terrorists. They are terrorists. Fear is their only strategy and it works.

Only when you've been there and done that, you're not so scared anymore, and you develop a few strategies of your own. You'll be prepared next time if there is one. It's easy to believe there will be a next time. There *has* to be so you can vindicate yourself for what happened this time. So in the process of preparation, you develop righteous anger. That righteous anger keeps you going while you replay in your mind how you will reclaim the rights these power-mongers have violated. The righteous anger keeps us in the role of the Survivor for as long as we find it useful. Unfortunately, it will also impede the healing process. Until we release the anger, even though we play the role of the Survivor, we will remain the Victim.

The final role we play in our various healing scenarios is that of the Champion. What vivid imagery comes to mind when you say the word—Champion. Yes, the champions, the ones with greatness in their hearts. They need not speak a word, because their deeds say it all. And so do yours. In this role, we accept our pain, our helplessness, and our victimization, as an opportunity to become greater than we were before it happened. We see our lives as a playing field. We will wear many uniforms, play many positions, win some, lose some, and learn, always learn. We need to learn so we can teach, and we need to teach, so we can continue to learn. We are the Champions! We are great!

We can share our greatness, the wisdom we've gained from our experiences, with those who are in their Victim and Survivor roles like we used to be. We can help them become Champions, too. So they can pass on the legacy of love that replaces the fear that creates the Victim that grows into the Champion.

CHAPTER FIFTEEN
THE VOICE OF GOD WHISPERS
TO OUR SACRED HEARTS

We come into this world with everything pure, of God, eager to learn and face anything that comes our way. All we need to accomplish our tasks here is love. We have come from a world of Pure Love, True Love, God's Love, and are thrust into a world of skepticism and doubt, of fear and judgment, and punishment. It's as if someone is saying, "I dare you to survive." But we have a very special tool, a secret code. We have our inner guidance. It is the voice of God whispering to our sacred hearts. We are connected. We need only to listen and trust our intuition and BE. The answers will come even before the questions are asked.

God does not want us to be poor. Poverty does not make us more spiritual. It makes us tired and discouraged, and we forget how to trust. It is important to remind ourselves of what we have and to be grateful for that. Gratefulness is one of the keys to Greatness. Every day, usually more than once, I say the following affirmations:

I release all fears and doubts.

I trust that my inner guidance will lead me to my dreams.

I am ready to accept wealth.

Saying this reminds me that it's okay to have good things in my life. It reminds me that I am worthy of good things and that I deserve to have a good life. So why not have a great life? We all deserve to be cared for and to be loved. I want to be reminded that only love can heal the pain I carry. It reminds me that I must let go of that pain if I am to manifest abundance in my life. The real burden is the heartache and sorrow we carry around with us. It is the emptiness we feel because we do not have enough love in our lives.

Where there is not enough love, fear springs up. Fear makes us feel isolated. Isolation kills dreams. When we feel isolated, it is easy to become discouraged, depressed, and even paranoid. We imagine all sorts of things. Our minds run rampant with the most ridiculous notions. Before we know it, our minds, which are wonderful servants, become our masters.

If you feel out of control, your mind is definitely in charge. Take back your life. Who you are is far more important than what you do. Yet the two are so connected that everything you do grows out of who you are.

There were some very turbulent years between my daughter and me when she was a teenager. They were chaotic because I knew nothing about being a parent. I knew what I learned from my mother, but that wasn't enough. I tried to follow the books, and do what all the experts said, but it didn't work for me.

I could have listened more to my heart and observed my child, so I could see what she needed, so I could know what she needed. But I didn't know how to do that so I allowed others to step in and call the shots. The outcome was not what either of us wanted.

I didn't learn about parenting until my daughter was living on her own. My friends thought I was crazy, but I wanted to know how to be a mother, even though my daughter was grown up. I wanted another chance someday. It may have been too late for us then, but I didn't want it to be too late for us later if I ever got another chance.

I believe that things happen as they're meant to and that my life is what it is because of the choices I've made. I can tell you this: Choosing love over fear doesn't sound tough, but it's the hardest thing I've ever done. And I still have to do it every day, and it's still hard. I have learned, though, that life is hard for everyone, even if it doesn't look that way to us.

We have to help each other heal, so we can heal. It's a team thing. Life is like that for the human race. Everybody finishes, and nobody gets out alive. When you look at it that way, it's really not a big deal. It's the right thing to do.

CHAPTER SIXTEEN
BE AN EXAMPLE

We are an example to those around us. If you finish high school, your children will probably finish high school. If you finish college, your children will probably go to college, too. They are empowered to finish school because it's been done already. Sure, Dad or Mom went to college. I guess I'll go too, no big deal. I never talked about college with my daughter when she was young. I didn't start college until after I was divorced, so I didn't really know much about it. And I didn't know how to talk about it because I'd never been there. My parents weren't college graduates, but I always wanted to go. I didn't know how to even ask about it. Then, one day I decided to do it, so I did. It took me a while but I finally got my degree. Then I could talk about it. It's not some big secret society, something that somebody else can have and you can't. It's just college for goodness sake, one more choice in your life. So if you want to go, go.

We are an example to those around us. Without uttering a word, we teach our children more than we realize. Adults often project their own unresolved fears onto their children. I could've shared some of my own life experiences with my daughter, but instead, I pretended my life was perfect and nothing bad ever happened to me. I could've guided her with love, and talked to her about life, but instead, I kept my mouth shut and let my fear guide me. We don't talk about those things with our children when we are in Victim and Survivor stages. They are still unresolved issues that make us feel ashamed and unworthy. We can learn to let them go, but it can take some time. Maybe the silence acts as a temporary fix. Or it could be those old fears life keeps waiting for us to let go of to make room for something better.

CHAPTER SEVENTEEN
WHERE DID I PUT MY LIFE?

One day I noticed that everybody else was in the painting of my life but me. And it was my life. Things were happening all around me, but I was missing out on all the fun. I was busy working hard so I could make a good life for myself and my daughter. And then I became painfully aware of something. I would put in months of work on a project, follow all the steps of a carefully orchestrated plan, or so I thought at the time, and I would get right to the threshold, and I'd stop. Since I was holding down a full-time job most of the time, it was years before I'd figured it out. I was trying to live my life from the outside looking in. I couldn't feel where I was supposed to be because I wasn't there.

I could make it happen for someone else, but not for me. The bottom line was I had taken my projects as far as I could take them. There wasn't anywhere else I could go with them. I had written the material and made the arrangements with the printer who would print the material. I made arrangements with the studio that was going to produce the material. I wrote the manuscripts. I sent out the query letters. I developed a marketing and distribution plan, and contacted magazines and publishers. The only thing I didn't do was to bring someone else in on the project to help me. I had a good reason for going it alone. I had been let down too many times before, and I didn't trust anybody to be there for me when it counted. I had been conditioned to believe that it was a weakness to ask for help.

And besides, you can't go out and ask for help from just anyone. You have to ask someone who is capable of helping you, someone who is in a position to help you, and someone who is willing to do the work. You have to ask the right people. But where do you find the right people? For instance, if your house is on fire, you wouldn't call a plumber even though plumbers have something to do with water. So did Moses, but he's not going to help you when your house is on fire. You call the fire department. Firefighters provide the kind and quantity of water you need in the way that you need it, to put out the flames in your burning house.

I asked the wrong people to help me. It was easier that way. My heart wasn't in it. Judgment and lack of trust cause resistance, and resisting what is makes you do stupid things. I chose people who didn't share my vision, who didn't have confidence in my ideas, who didn't have the money to help me finance my projects, and who didn't want to work. They thought it would be nice to be around me just in case I made it, so that they can say they knew me when. What I needed was synergy, that blast of creative power that happens when you combine energy from different sources. It's that collective radiance that makes two plus two equal ten. Options and solutions seem to come out of nowhere when people put their creative minds together and brainstorm impossibilities. I couldn't make that happen by myself. I needed other people and I needed to take action.

CHAPTER EIGHTEEN
CAN I GET SOME HELP OVER HERE?

You know what I finally did to get help? I asked my friends. I asked people who I knew who were acquaintances. I asked people they referred me to. I was amazed at how my small circle of friends was able to help me by sharing information they had. They put me in touch with people they knew. I had no idea these folks I saw on a regular basis were so well connected. You see, the information they had wasn't valuable to them. There was never any reason to share it with me until I shared my plan with them. That's when it started to come together. I was astounded. I thought it was some big ordeal—it had been up to this point. But this time I started small, and let the flower unfold naturally. It took talking about my idea, not giving it away, just letting people who were in positions to help me, get caught up in it, the way my English teacher got caught up in my stories. And it worked.

How many times have you reached that point in your life? Maybe it was a project, or relationship, a great job. Or it was something you were trying to buy, or a trip you wanted to take. And you tried to do everything yourself. Did you really enjoy it? Was it all it could've been? We fool ourselves in so many ways by convincing ourselves we did all we could do, but..... Hear that "but" at the end? That's how you know you didn't do all you could do. You could've asked for help.

We have to try a few impossible things once in a while, stretch a little, use our imagination, and dream. You never know what you can do until you do it, and do it, and do it. Sometimes it takes impossible means to make things happen. For me it seemed impossible to find somebody who would give me the money to run ads and pay for printing. As it turned out, I found three people who were more than willing to help me get started. It seemed impossible to find a person who I could actually talk to about my idea and who would say "Sure, it will work, Bernie. You are going to be great at this. People will love to listen to you." As it turned out, I found several, and they all came to my first seminar. But I wasn't finished whining yet.

Then I was worried that people might not want to pay to come to my seminars. It stressed me out so much that I charged bargain basement rates, and did lots of free stuff, just to get the word out so that people would know who I was. I didn't realize it at the time, but the value of what I had to share had been diminished in my own eyes by all the free stuff. I had confused price with value. And what did the people who came to my seminar say to me afterwards? "This would've been cheap at twice the price." "You should've charged more." "I really got a lot out of this." Sometimes a person would stuff ten dollars, or sometimes twenty dollars in my pocket or my purse. "Take this, you deserve it," they would say. "You've helped me so much."

And I thought, "My goodness gracious, if they value my work like this, then who am *I*, who *am* I to insult them by saying, 'Oh it was nothing'." It was definitely something! The only one who hadn't recognized that yet was me.

I was still learning how to be okay with receiving expressions of gratitude when I shared my gift with people. Once I began to place more value on my work, as others had, I was able to invite outsiders into my sphere, my inner circle, to help me accomplish what I wanted to accomplish. I was able to finish existing projects so I could begin new ones, so I could happen to life. I found younger people, and older people, people who were capable and talented but, for one reason or another, had not been successful in their environments. I brought them into projects and they thrived. Why did they thrive? Because they were just like me. They were talented and skilled, but they got to the threshold and they stopped because they were scared. They couldn't run away fast enough and they didn't want to talk about it.

Now here we were talking about it, creating stories and ideas, and it wasn't scary anymore. And it didn't seem so impossible anymore. We helped each other.

The things that seemed like obstacles before got lost in all the ideas. It was incredible, and the synergy—WOW! It was happening. We were happening to life. We started talking about dreams and ideas, brainstorming, and talking about things that mattered. You start doing that and you find out they matter to the person next to you, the person in front of you, and you realize, that those dreams belong to everyone.

Nobody owns a dream. The things I want out of my life, are the things hundreds and thousands of people want out of their lives. We each have our own unique way of spreading love and eradicating fear in the world. And that world starts right here, with us, our families, and our communities. It starts with the people we love and care about. And then it trickles down or explodes into the rest of the world to be available to anyone else who also cares about it.

The world is ready whenever we are. Life is waiting for us, beckoning, shouting at us, "It's Never Too Late to Be Great!"

CHAPTER NINETEEN
WHEN DO YOU KNOW?

Many years ago when I first read Napoleon Hill's book, "Think and Grow Rich", I took exception to his saying that most people don't really become successful until they're in their forties. I said, "Oh no, oh no, no. I know what I'm going to do." I was in my twenties then. And then my thirties came and went. And when I was forty, I knew what he was talking about. I learned that you have to fall down so you can learn how to get up. That you need to crawl before you can walk. There's a certain order of things, a sequence that must be followed in order to create a strong foundation so that we can fall, brace ourselves, get up, brush off, and do it again and again until it works for us.

Don't ever give up! There are so many things we have to experience in our lives, so many actions we will have to take, and so many decisions we will have to make. They don't affect just us. They affect everyone. They affect the entire universe and they start with us. Mine start with me. Yours start with you.

There is nothing to be afraid of out there. And there is everything to be afraid of out there. It's all unknown. The best thing we can do for ourselves is to be the best people we can be. Take it all in. Find what works for you and let the rest go.

Be honest. And I don't mean be honest as in, I don't lie and I don't cheat and I don't steal because everyone does in some way, shape, or form. That's just the way it is. Eventually, that stuff works itself out. It's the little stuff. I'm talking about being honest with yourself.

Become excellent at changing your mind. When you realize you're doing something you don't feel comfortable doing, stop and start over. Or do something else. You've heard that definition of insanity—doing the same thing over and over and expecting a different result. Change your mind, and take a new picture. Find out what's going on around you. Get to know the people you work with and live next door to. Give yourself the opportunity to have a different viewpoint. We have to feel the fear so we can let it go, so we can let the love in, and so we can remember why we are here. So we can be what we came here to be and do what we came here to do, right here, right now.

Happen to life. Life is ever-changing. And all the things you can say about life, and change, comes down to one thing. All the things you want from your life, whether you get them or not, come down to one thing: WHO YOU ARE. Who you are is what you get.

And if who you are is great, then what you get will be great. And what you do with it will be great. And it won't be great because of *it*. It will be great because of you.

Right here, right now, in this very spot, you can choose. You don't *need* to, but you *can*.

Grab a mirror!

I choose to be myself.

I am perfect just the way I am.

I like who I am right now, and I like who I am becoming.

When I need help, I will ask for it.

If I cannot get the help I need from the first person I ask, I will keep asking until I get what I need to finish the job.

I will *fearlessly* share my ideas, and I will help others become the best they can be by being the best *I* can be. And the best I can be is who I am.

That is what greatness is all about. It's about being who you are. It's about being that Divine Spark of energy, that essence of life, that perfect self we see through our imperfect eyes. Take a better look. Take a new picture.

CHAPTER TWENTY
JUST LUCKY, I GUESS? GUESS AGAIN.

We create our own luck. The choices we make determine our timing and our luck. As we get to know ourselves better, we will make better choices that will make our lives better for us. We can change our unhappiness by changing our attitude toward our lives, by changing our attitude towards ourselves. Life will return to us what we give to it.

You can create the life you want by enjoying what you already have. By saying "thank you" more than "please". By letting things be so they can fall into place naturally. Doing is good. *Being* is better. There is no need to force a flower to bloom before it is ready. Enjoy your life. It's your turn now. Now will never come again.

Live a meaningful life with people in it that you want to be there. Make friends with the Victim, Survivor, and Champion parts of yourself. Love and accept yourself. You are perfect just the way you are.

Feel the fear and let it go. Find the love and let it flow. Step across that threshold into the life you have created for yourself. Happen to Life! And find out for yourself what in your heart of hearts you always knew was true……..

That…………… **It's Never Too Late to Be Great!**

Share the Transformative Power that Believing and Never Giving Up Can Have for You Regardless of Your Age or Life Circumstances

You now know that you have the ability to achieve your dreams and thrive in a wonderful life where age and life circumstances mean less than being who you are. And the time has come to show other readers where they can find the same encouragement and inspiration.

Simply by leaving your honest opinion of this book on Amazon, you'll show other dreamers like yourself that there is always the opportunity for personal fulfillment if you are willing to believe, have hope, do the work, and never give up.

Thank you for your help. You can encourage other adults to discover that just because your life has been one way up until now doesn't mean it has to stay that way. You can make your dreams come true at any age and find joy just by being your own perfect self.

https://www.amazon.com/review/create-review/?channel=glance-detail&asin=096620493X&ie=UTF8

ABOUT THE AUTHOR

 BERNADETTE GREGGORY is an author, Holistic Wellness Consultant, and avid aviation enthusiast. She has been a personal empowerment trainer, an award-winning medical radio talk show host, a business management consultant, and a child development trainer. Her other interests include music and Nature. She believes that daily life can bring great joy and fulfillment to anyone who is courageous enough to live life with an open mind and heart.

www.ingramcontent.com/pod-product-compliance
Lightning Source LLC
Chambersburg PA
CBHW031428290426
44110CB00011B/575